Victoria Roberts is a specialist in Business and Property matters with a particular leaning to the mis-selling of financial services. She practises in consumer loans and car finance up to Supreme Court level. Victoria has previously worked as In-House Counsel for the Financial Conduct Authority.

Nick Harrison is a Business and Property Barrister. His practice includes a broad mix of chancery, commercial and sports law work. He specialises in financial mis-selling claims.

A Practical Guide to the Mis-Selling of Car Finance

A Practical Guide to the Mis-Selling of Car Finance

Victoria Roberts
Barrister, Lincoln's Inn
18 St John Street Chambers, Manchester

Nick Harrison
Barrister, Middle Temple
18 St John Street Chambers, Manchester

Law Brief Publishing

Published 2025 by Law Brief Publishing, an imprint of Law Brief Publishing Ltd
30 The Parks
Minehead
Somerset
TA24 8BT

www.lawbriefpublishing.com

Paperback: 978-1-914608-61-2

PREFACE

This is the first book of its kind in respect of the financial mis-selling of car finance. We consider that this book provides an outline of the law in this area to date which is a fast-moving area. The law is stated as at 17 January 2025.

I am grateful to my co-author, Nick Harrison for agreeing to assist me with this exciting publication, the first one of its kind. I dedicate this book to Peter, Elin, David and Joanne.

Victoria Roberts
January 2025

I am delighted to have worked on this publication with my friend and colleague, Victoria Roberts. I dedicate this book to Gilli, Henry and Florence.

Nick Harrison
January 2025

CONTENTS

CHAPTER ONE

INTRODUCTION – TYPES OF CAR FINANCE AGREEMENTS

1. In the context of car purchasing, a customer usually purchases the car from a car dealership and the car dealership offers to find car finance on behalf of the consumer. Car dealers (brokers) must generally be an authorised representative for these purposes if they are offering credit to a prospective customer[1]. Upon being authorised, the car dealer will need to demonstrate that it can comply with the FCA's Principles of Business, comply with the FCA's Handbook Rules and the FCA's Threshold Conditions[2].

2. Most car finance agreements will generally be credit agreements regulated by the Consumer Credit Act 1974. A consumer credit agreement is defined under the Consumer Credit Act as an

> "*agreement between an individual ("the debtor") and any other person ("the creditor") by which the creditor provides*

[1,2] The FCA's full credit authorisation regime applies to all "high-risk" consumer credit lending activities which include credit brokerage. The FCA's threshold conditions would require the car dealership to show that it is "*ready, willing and organised*" by demonstrating that it has appropriate resources, a business model, effective supervision, having its offices within the United Kingdom and is suitable to be authorised: see the FCA's threshold conditions, Paragraphs 2D to 2F of Schedule 6 FSMA 2000, The Financial Services and Markets Act 2000). See also Chapter Two below.

credit of any amount[3]. *Credit can include a cash loan and any other form of financial accommodation*[4].

For agreements after 1 April 2014.....

A regulated agreement can include a hire agreement or a credit agreement".

3. For regulatory purposes, the Financial Conduct Authority, who took on the regulation of motor finance and consumer credit firms in April 2014, adopts the wording of Article 60B of the Regulated Activities Order[5] in its definition of consumer credit lending as "*entering into a regulated credit agreement as lender, or having the right to exercise, the lender's rights and duties under a regulated credit agreement*".

4. For common law purposes, the definition provided by s.8(1) of the CCA 1974 has been applied by the courts when defining what a consumer credit agreement is[6]. The case of *Diamond v Lovell* referenced the definition of credit in the book, Goode Consumer Credit Legislation as:

"*credit [is] extended whenever the contract provides for the debtor to pay, or gives him the option to pay, later than the*

---

3 S.8(1) of the Consumer Credit Act 1974. See also Article 60B of the Regulated Activities Order 2001

4 S.9(1) of the Consumer Credit Act 1974

5 The Financial Services and Markets Act 2000 (Regulated Activities Order) 2001

6 Durkin v DSG Retail Ltd and another [2014[UKSC 21. See also Diamond v Lovell [1993] 3 All ER 1

time at which payment would have been earned under the express or the implied terms of the contract".[7]

5. In the context of car finance, most agreements are "restricted use agreements"[8] which usually involves the consumer purchasing a vehicle pursuant to a hire-purchase or PCP agreement. The key feature of a restricted use agreement is that the borrower is not free to use the credit for any purpose they wish.

6. For the purposes of car finance agreements, the main types of agreements are:

<u>Hire-purchase agreement</u>

This is where the customer pays for the finance by way of instalments over a fixed period of time. Some agreements offer a "balloon payment" whereby the customer pays a final amount in order to become the owner of the vehicle (normally through the

---

7 Goode Consumer Credit Legislation 1999, vol 1, para 433, Diamond v Lovell at p572

8 See s.11(a)-(b) of the CCA 1974 which states that:

A restricted-use agreement is a regulated consumer credit agreement –

(a) To finance a transaction between the debtor and the creditor, whether forming part of that agreement or not, or

(b) To finance a transaction between the debtor and a person ("the supplier) other than the creditor……

(c) An agreement does not fall subsection (1) if the credit is in fact provided in such a way as to leave the debtor free to use it as he chooses, even though certain uses would contravene that or any other agreement.

option of "an option to purchase fee"). In such a scenario, lenders will sometimes offer a guaranteed future value for the vehicle which is linked to the balloon payment. Conversely, conditional sale agreements procure that the borrower automatically owns the goods once the final payment has been made.

PCP (personal contract purchase) agreement

Usually a customer would pay a deposit and then pay the finance agreement by way of monthly instalments (usually based upon an amount the lender thinks the car will lose in value over the period of the agreement less the customer's deposit). At the end of the agreement, the customer can either pay a final balloon payment or they can use what equity they have built up in the vehicle to put towards as a deposit for the purchase of a new vehicle. In these types of agreements, there will sometimes be annual mileage restrictions attached to the agreement.[9]

Lease-hire

Under such an agreement, the customer agrees to rent the vehicle and return it at the end of a specified period.

9 A statutory consideration such as s.100(1) CCA 1974 which may apply to such mileage restrictions in a voluntary termination scenario.

CHAPTER TWO

REGULATORY OBLIGATIONS OF INTERMEDIARIES (CAR DEALERS)

7. Car dealers (which generally operate as credit brokers)[10] must conduct their business within the confines of the wide-ranging Consumer Rights Act 2015. Some relevant considerations for car dealers under the CRA 2015 ("CRA") are:

    (i) The vehicle must be fit for purpose;

    (ii) of satisfactory quality;

    (iii) as described.

8. Any contractual terms which fall foul of the CRA may be subject to an unfairness claim under s.140A of the Consumer Credit Act 1974.

9. Car dealers must also comply with other statutory obligations such as the Consumer Protection from Unfair Trading Regulations 2008[11], the Consumer Rights (Payment of Surcharges) Regulations 2012 and the Consumer Contracts (Information, Cancellation and Additional Charges Regulations) 2013.

---

[10] As defined by Article 36A of the Financial Services and Markets Act 2000 (Regulated Activities Order 2001)

[11] These regulations will be substantially revoked when the Digital Markets Competition Consumers Act 2024 comes into force.

10. There are various trade bodies which assist car dealers such as Retail Motor Industry Federation which is an associate of The National Franchised Dealers Association.

11. There are also various associations which aim to support intermediaries who offer motor finance[12]. The Finance and Leasing Association ('FLA') operates a code of practice[13] which requires intermediary members amongst other things:

    (i) *"not to pressurise customers to enter into any agreement and try to make sure that credit brokers, and all other suppliers of goods and services [the FLA] does business with do not pressurise customers"*[14].

12. In order to become authorised by the FCA in the first place, car dealers must meet the FCA's threshold conditions to show that they are "ready, willing and organised"[15] at the time of approval which include satisfying the FCA of some of the following conditions:

[12] See for example, The Financial Intermediary and Broker Association, Finance and Leasing Association, The National Association of Commercial Finance Brokers, British Vehicle Rental and Leasing Association

[13] FLA Lending Code 2021

[14] See Paragraph 1A.1, FLA Lending Code 2021

[15] See Paragraphs 2B to 2F of The Financial Services and Markets Act (Threshold Conditions) Order 2013 / COND 2.2-2.6

(i) *For the "mind and management" of the Firm*[16] *to be in the UK;*

(ii) *The Firm must have effective supervision with sufficient controllers / affiliates;*

(iii) *The Firm must have appropriate financial / non-financial resources;*

(iv) *The Firm must demonstrate that the senior leaders of the Firm are "fit and proper" persons;*

(v) *The Firm's business model can be conducted in a sound and prudent manner.*

13. In relation to commission arrangements held between car dealers and lenders, historically, the OFT[17] provided guidance to credit brokers and intermediaries which included a transparency requirement about fees received by a credit broker both from the borrower and lender. For example, the OFT expected brokers to provide details about the existence of a commission if that commission may have potentially impacted on the impartiality of the broker in respect of the credit products it offered to a borrower. At that time, the OFT considered that:

> *"a person [intermediary] would be unlikely to be considered independent if he gave preference to particular products (for*

---

16 Firm is defined by the FCA as "an authorised person including an applicant for a Part 4A permission (COND) but not a professional firm unless it is an authorised professional firm".

17 "the OFT Credit Broker Guidance", November 2011

> *example, because of differential commission rates, volume over-riders or other benefits*)"[18].

14. Presently, once authorised, intermediaries must comply with the FCA's Rule Handbook known as 'CONC'[19] and the FCA's recently implemented Consumer Duty[20].

15. Some of the relevant CONC Rules applicable to car dealers in the context of secret commissions paid by lenders are as follows:

    Conc Rule 4.5.3R where credit brokers are "required to disclose to a customer in good time before a credit agreement is entered into[21], the existence and nature of any commission or fee or other remuneration payable to the credit broker by the lender where the existence or amount of the commission, fee or other remuneration could actually or potentially:

    > "(1) *affect the impartiality of the credit broker in recommending the credit agreement*[22]*…; or*

---

18 OFT1307con, p 26-27

19 Consumer Credit Sourcebook

20 Implemented on 31 July 2023

21 See also CONC 3.3.1R which requires a firm to ensure that a communication or a financial promotion is clear, fair, and not misleading.

22 See also CONC 2.5.8(13)R (a credit broker must not give preference to credit products of a lender where the object of doing so it to make a personal gain) and CONC 3.7.3R (a credit broker must indicate the extent of its powers and in particular whether it works exclusively with one or more lenders or works independently) and CONC 3.7.4G (under (2) a credit broker must indicate to the

(2) if made known to the customer, have a material impact on the customer's transactional decision to enter into the credit agreement..."

Note: paragraph 3.7i (box) and 3.7j of CBG[23] and 5.5 (box) of ILG[24].

16. The effect of paragraph 3.7i(box) and 3.7j of CBG[25] was that the OFT said that:

(i) potential borrowers should be made aware of the existence of a financial arrangement between a broker and a creditor that might potentially impact on the impartiality of the broker in terms of the credit products that it promoted to a potential borrower, or when knowledge of the existence or amount of commission could potentially have a material impact on the potential borrower's borrowing decision;

(ii) the amount or likely amount of any commission should be disclosed by the broker on request by the borrower so that the borrower should be enabled to take a view as to whether there was likely to be a conflict of interest.

---

customer in a prominent way the existence of any financial arrangements with a lender that might impact upon the firm's impartiality in promoting a credit product to a customer).

23 OFT's Credit and Intermediaries Guidance

24 OFT's Irresponsible Lending Guide

25 The Office of Fair Trading's Credit Brokers and Intermediaries Guidance published in November 2011

> *Failure to do these things was an unfair or improper business practice.*

17. In relation to CONC 4.5.3R, the FCA said in paragraphs 3.28 to 3.31 of its Motor Finance Final Findings[26] that:

> "*Our rules in CONC 4.5.3R require brokers to disclose, in good time before a credit agreement is entered into, the existence of any commission or fee or other remuneration payable to the broker by a lender (or a third party) if knowledge of the existence or amount of the commission could actually or potentially:*
>
> *(i) affect the broker's impartiality in recommending a particular product; or*
>
> *(ii) have a material impact on the customer's transactional decision*
>
> "*This would include DiC*[27] *and similar commission arrangements which allow the broker discretion to adjust the interest rate, to earn more commission. This is a conflict of interest that may affect the broker's impartiality. It may also affect the customer's decision on whether to deal with the broker or to proceed to an agreement. If the customer is aware of the existence of such arrangements, they can take this into account, and probe further if they want or request an*

26 Page 15

27 Difference in charges

indication of the amount or likely amount of the commission (which the broker must provide upon request)". [28]

18. CONC 3.7.4G(2) states that:

> "*A firm should in a financial promotion or in a communication with a customer:*
>
> *indicate to the customer in a prominent way the existence and nature of any financial arrangements with a lender that might impact upon the firm's impartiality in promoting or recommending a credit product to the customer or which might, if disclosed by the firm to the customer, affect the customer's transactional decision in relation to the credit product".*

Note: paragraphs 2.2, 6th bullet and 4.6 of the CBG[29]. Paragraph 2.2 of the CBG[30] sets out the principles expected of credit brokers and intermediaries which states that they should, where applicable:

---

[28] See also the FOS ' Ombudsman decision of Re L, DRN-4326581 (which was later subject to a judicial review challenge in the case of *R (on the application of Clydesdale Financial Services Limited v Financial Ombudsman Service Limited (Arnold Clark Automobiles Limited, Jenna Lewis and the Financial Conduct Authority as interested parties) [2024] EWHC 3237 (Admin)*

[29] The Office of Fair Trading's Credit Brokers and Intermediaries Guidance 2011

[30] OFT1307con

(i) ensure transparency in all dealings with borrowers and they should not use misleading or oppressive behaviour, including when advertising or otherwise promoting consumer credit or hire agreements. This would include – but not be limited to – all advertising and marketing materials, web-sites and pre- contract information;

(ii) ensure information and documentation directed at, or provided to, borrowers, is compliant with relevant legislative requirements;

(iii) not provide advice (where advice is given) or information (including documentary information) that is unsuitable or inappropriate given the borrower's circumstances;

(iv) clearly disclose their status (including any links with creditors) and the level of service offered;

(v) provide full and early disclosure of any fees payable by the borrower, setting out what the fees are for, when and how they are payable, and any provisions for refunds, including in accordance with the requirements of section 155 of the CCA 1974;

(vi) treat borrowers fairly – borrowers should not be targeted with credit products that are clearly unsuitable for them, or subjected to aggressive or oppressive behaviour or coercion. Neither should they be subjected to conduct that is deceitful, oppressive, unfair or improper, whether unlawful or not. Borrowers who may be particularly vulnerable by virtue of their current indebtedness, poor credit history, or by reason of age or health, or disability, or for any other reason, should, in particular, not be targeted or exploited;

(vii) where appropriate, provide early disclosure of information relating to, and explanation of, key features of the credit agreement, including key risks to the borrower, to better enable borrowers to make informed choices.

19. CONC 3.3.1R states that:

"A firm must ensure that a communication or a financial promotion is clear, fair, and not misleading."

20. Further, pursuant to CONC 4.5.4R, a broker must disclose the amount (or likely amount) of commission to the customer in good time before a regulated agreement is entered into if the customer asks. In practice, this Rule is likely to only apply in situations where a customer has been informed that a commission *may* be payable in the contractual documents or otherwise. [31]

21. On 28 January 2021[32], the FCA introduced CONC rules 4.5.5G and 4.5.6R which prohibits car dealers from using discretionary commission arrangements (DCAs) i.e. an arrangement whereby credit brokers are given authority by the lender to decide or negotiate the price of a regulated agreement in order to achieve the

---

31 In the recent Court of Appeal decision of *Johnson v First Rand Bank Ltd (T/A Motonovo Finance [2024] EWCA Civ 1282*, the Court clarified that a commission is either secret or it in not. It is the extent of disclosure given that may negate the secrecy: see Paragraph 11. Thus, by giving the customer this information may amount to "partial disclosure", which will negate secrecy (and thus a finding of bribery) but may still amount to a breach of fiduciary duty.

32 See also the FCA's Report on Motor Finance – Final Findings 2019: https://www.fca.org.uk/publication/multi-firm-reviews/our-work-on-motor-finance-final-findings.pdf

commission or remuneration payable to the broker by the lender. The relevant commission arrangements which therefore currently remain permissible between car dealers and lenders are fixed[33] and scaled[34] commission structures. The FCA is currently undertaking a review pursuant to its powers under s.166 FSMA 2000. The ambit of this review is to consider historical motor finance arrangements involving DCAs and sales across several lenders. If the review finds widespread misconduct across the car finance market then one possible outcome for the FCA would be to introduce an redress scheme which will apply across the market to compensate consumers. [35]

22. In some circumstances, breaches of regulatory rules can result in an award for damages for breach of statutory duty under s.138D(2) of the Financial Services and Markets Act 2000 ('FSMA'),[36] which states that:

> *"A contravention by an authorised person of a rule made by the FCA is actionable at the suit of a private person who suffers loss as a result of the contravention, subject to the*

33 Usually a fixed amount i.e. a percentage of the total amount of finance borrowed which is paid to the car dealer by the lender.

34 Also known as a variable product fee where the car dealer is paid a fee which varies (within parameters) according to the interest rate attached to the regulated agreement.

35 Any redress scheme will be subject to a consultation. See Inside FCA Podcast: Interview with Nikhil Rathi on the review of the Motor Finance Market, 1 August 2024, p2

36 See Haider Abdullah v Credit Suisse [2017] EWHC 3016 (Comm)

defences and other incidents applying to actions for breach of statutory duty".[37]

23. In summary, there are clear obligations on car dealers to communicate to customers in a way which is fair and not misleading. Chapter three considers in more detail about how the Court of Appeal viewed the commission disclosures (where relevant) in *Johnson, Wrench and Hopcraft*[38] particularly with regard to the "prominence" of an express partial commission term in a contractual document.

Regulatory Obligations of Lenders

24. A lender under a regulated credit agreement is subject to certain rules within CONC under Article 60B(1) Financial Services and Markets Act (Regulated Activities Order) 2000.

25. Lenders are required to comply with the FCA's Principles of Business. Relevant principles in a car finance lending context include requirements that Firms:

    (i) conduct its business with due skill;[39]

[37] As considered in some PCP county court decisions such as: Prendergast v BMW (2021) Bradford County Court, Fudge v Black Horse Limited (2022) Basingstoke County Court

[38] *Johnson v First Rand Bank Ltd (T/A Motonovo Finance [2024] EWCA Civ 1282*

[39] Principle 2

(ii) Communicate with customers in a way that is clear, fair and not misleading[40]

(iii) Manage conflicts of interest fairly both between the lender and the customer and another client;[41]

(iv) Take reasonable care to ensure the suitability of its advice and suitability of its advice and discretionary decisions for any customer who is entitled to rely upon its judgment;[42]

(v) Deliver good outcomes for retail customers.[43].

26. The following CONC duties are likely to be applicable to lenders in the context of car finance sales:

CONC 1.2.2R states:

"A firm[44] must:

(1) Ensure that its employees and agents comply CONC; and

(2) Take reasonable steps to ensure that other persons acting on its behalf comply with CONC."

---

40 Principle 7... n.b from 31 July 2023, Principles 6 and 7 were disapplied in favour of the Consumer Duty found in PRIN 2A.1.17G(1)).

41 Principle 8

42 Principle 9

43 Principle 12

44 An authorised person (i.e. a person who has a Part 4A permission as defined under s.55A FSMA 2000) but not a professional firm

27. One argument in relation to this CONC Rule, may be that lenders should take reasonable steps to ensure, that the car dealer has complied with its obligations under CONC regarding commission disclosure.

28. CONC 2.3.2R states that:

> *"A firm must explain the key features of a regulated credit agreement to enable the customer to make an informed choice as required by CONC 4.2.5R(adequate explanations)."*

29. The lender or car dealer is required to give the adequate explanations to the customer either orally or in writing[45]. In some cases therefore, lenders sometimes outline key financial information on a separate information sheet[46].

30. Lenders are required to carry out a "reasonable" credit worthiness assessment pursuant to CONC 5.2.A.4R. Under the Rules, this requires a lender to:

    (i) Base its creditworthiness assessment on sufficient information it has at the time the creditworthiness assessment has been carried out[47];

---

45 CONC 4.2.5(3)R

46 This information must be provided in good time before the customer signs the regulated agreement and the customer should have the opportunity to take the pre-contractual information away with them (See: Consumer Credit (Disclosure of Information) Regulations 2010)

47 See CONC 5.2A.7(1). Sufficient information is not defined within the FCA's Handbook Rules

(ii) Where appropriate, obtain such information from the customer and where necessary from a credit reference agency[48];

(iii) Consider the consumer's ability to make the repayments on their due dates[49] and the risk to the customer of not being able to meet the repayments under the agreement[50]. In order to determine this, the lender must be satisfied that such repayments can be made from one of the following[51]:

- The customer's income;
- Income from savings or assets held by the customer or jointly with another person;
- Without the customer having to borrow to meet such repayments;
- Without the customer failing to meet any of its other contractual or statutory obligations;
- Without such repayments having a significant adverse impact on the customer's financial situation.

---

48 See CONC 5.2A.7(2)

49 See CONC 5.2A.10(1)

50 See CONC 5.2A.10(2)

51 See CONC 5.2A.12(1-5)

31. The Financial Ombudsman has published some decisions[52] relating to inadequate affordability assessments carried out by lenders in car finance cases in situations where customers stated that the repayments were unaffordable. In the complaint of Mr A the Ombudsman upheld a complaint and determined that Santander Consumer (UK) Plc irresponsibly provided a conditional sale agreement for the purchase of a car by failing to carry out a sufficiently thorough reasonable and proportionate assessment of Mr A's ability to repay the agreement.

32. Further in its Report of the Motor Industry[53], the FCA noted in its findings that:

> *"In 7 cases, the firms' processes seemed generally satisfactory. However, there were gaps or ambiguities in the information provided, and elements of the assessment were unclear. In particular, it was not always clear what information or data would be used in an assessment, or whether and how this might be verified, particularly in marginal cases. It was also unclear how indicators of affordability risk would be taken into account, according to the costs and risks to the individual customer, and how these were reflected in metrics used.*
>
> *In 8 cases, we did not have enough information to assess compliance with CONC. The firms' responses did not provide sufficient details of the process used, or how this might vary depending upon the product and customer. For example, it was unclear how policy rules or scorecards would operate (particularly where processes were automated) to decide*

---

[52] See for example Re R DRN-3224900, Re A DRN-2238722, Re T DRN-4511519, Re M DRN-4394165

[53] 2019

whether applications were accepted or rejected or referred to manual underwriting. In most cases firms appeared to rely on a mix of applicant information plus data from credit reference agencies (CRAs). However, it was not always clear which CRA products were being used, and in what ways, or what might trigger asking the customer for documentary evidence"[54].

33. In relation to the FCA's requirements imposed on lenders regarding secret commissions, CONC 4.5.2 provides that a lender should only offer a firm a commission agreement where such payments are justified based on the extra work of the firm involved. Further a claim for mis-selling may be founded in circumstances where it is held that the broker has breached CONC 4.5.3 as to a broker being required to disclose the existence and nature of a commission to a customer[55]. Further, lenders are also required to ensure that car dealers complies with the CONC 1.2.2R.

34. The Courts at County Court level have taken into such regulatory breaches in claims for unfairness under s.140A of the CCA 1974[56]. In the County Court case of Beckett v BMW[57], HHJ Sykes on appeal granted the claimant an award under s.140B CCA 1974 by finding that a DCA model of commission creates a conflict of

---

54 See Paragraphs 5.6 and 5.7

55 See Chapter Two

56 *see* Kerrigan v Elevate Credit International Limited (t/a Sunny) (in administration) *[2020] EWHC 2169 (Comm) and Jones v BMW [2023] at paragraph 75.* Such could be considered alongside a cause of action under s.138D FSMA 2000

57 [2021] Liverpool County Court

interest as found by the FCA in its report[58]. Most recently, in the conjoined Court of Appeal decision of *Johnson v FirstRand Bank Limited T/A Motonovo Finance*[59] ("*Johnson, Wrench and Hopcraft*"), a case which at first instance considered breaches of CONC Rules 2.5.8(13) R and 3.7.4G[60], the Court held that:

> "*a relationship will not necessarily be unfair for the purposes of the 1974 Act simply because a broker receives commission from the lender and the borrower is not actually aware of that fact. The court is to consider all the facts and to weigh their importance. If the commission is very high in relation to the sum borrowed, that may, in itself, be enough to make the relationship unfair where nothing, or nothing of substance, has been done to disclose the relationship between the lender and the broker.*"[61]

58 Paragraph 57 of the note of judgment

59 and others [2024] EWCA Civ 1282

60 In the *Johnson* element of the appeal

61 Paragraph 170

CHAPTER THREE

SECRET COMMISSIONS JURISPRUDENCE

35. The modern law of the tort of bribery was developed in a series of cases in the late 19th and early 20th centuries. The key principles were summed up as a three-fold test by Slade J in *Industries & General Mortgage Co Ltd v Lewis*[62] [1949] 2 All ER 573 ("*Lewis*"):

> *"For the purposes of the civil law a bribe means the payment of a secret commission, which only means*
>
> *(i) that the person making the payment makes it to the agent of the other person with whom he is dealing;*
>
> *(ii) that he makes it to that person knowing that that person is acting as the agent of the other person with whom he is dealing; and*
>
> *(iii) that he fails to disclose to the other person with whom he is dealing that he has made that payment to the person whom he knows to be the other person's agent.*
>
> *Those three are the only elements necessary to constitute the payment of a secret commission or bribe for civil purposes."*

36. The *Lewis* three-fold test has been cited in numerous subsequent reported cases, including, recently, the Court of Appeal's decision

62 [1949] 2 All ER 573

in *Wood v Commercial First Business Ltd; Business Mortgage Finance 4 plc v Pengelly*[63] ("*Wood/Pengelly*"). The *Wood / Pengelly* decision was also considered most recently in the *Johnson, Wrench and Hopcraft* decision. Nonetheless, all of its elements require further explanation and reference to case law, for otherwise the *dicta* quoted above, taken at face value, give a misleadingly narrow impression of the circumstances in which the tort of bribery can be made out. The meaning of "bribe" or "commission", and the nature of the relationship between the principal and the "agent", will be considered in this chapter as will the requirement for non-disclosure of the payment to the principal.

Meaning of "bribe" or "commission"

37. It is not necessary for there to be a payment of a "commission" as defined in everyday language, i.e. a corrupt payment, typically by way of reward for arranging a particular transaction. In *Hovenden and Sons v Millhoff*[64], Romer LJ stated that:

> *'The courts of law of this country have always strongly condemned and, when they could, punished the bribing of agents, and have taken a strong view as to what constitutes a bribe... Without attempting an exhaustive definition, I may say that the following is one statement of what constitutes a bribe. If a gift be made to a confidential agent with the view of inducing the agent to act in favour of the donor in relation to transactions between the donor and the agent's principal and that gift is secret as between the donor and the agent—*

63 [2021] EWCA Civ 471

64 (1900) 83 LT 41

that is to say, without the knowledge and consent of the principal—then the gift is a bribe in the view of the law.'

38. It follows that, for the purposes of civil remedies, the meaning of "bribe" extends well beyond its popular connotation of a corrupt payment, to include any payment or gift made as an inducement to an "agent" and not disclosed to the "principal".[65]

39. The use of a broad definition of "bribe" stems from the fact that an undisclosed conflict of interest is a fundamental element of the tort of bribery. This was established by the leading nineteenth century authority, *Panama and South Pacific Telegraph Co v India Rubber, Gutta Percha and Telegraph Works Co*[66] ("Panama Telegraph"). The claimant company contracted with the defendant company to lay a submarine cable. The claimant hired an engineer to certify progress of the works and agreed to pay him percentage commissions on its contractual payments to the defendant as and when they were made. Unbeknown to the claimant, the engineer was also hired by the defendant company to supervise the laying of the cable. When the claimant discovered this fact, it sought to rescind its contract with the defendant company and recover the payments it had made thereunder, and it also sought repayment of the commissions it had made under its contract with the engineer.

65 See also *Wood* at Paragraph 43

66 (1875) LR 10 Ch App 515

40. The High Court and Court of Appeal allowed the claimant's claim. In the Court of Appeal, James LJ stated the applicable principle as follows[67]:

> *"According to my view of the law of this court, I take it to be clear that any surreptitious dealing between one principal and the agent of the other principal is a fraud on such other principal, cognizable in this court. That I take to be a clear proposition, and I take it, according to my view, to be equally clear that the defrauded principal, if he comes in time, is entitled, at his option, to have the contract rescinded, or, if he elects not to have it rescinded, to have such other adequate relief as the court may think right to give him."*

41. Applying this proposition to the facts of *Panama Telegraph*, the claimant was entitled to the impartial advice of the engineer, but the engineer's undisclosed contract with the defendant company put him in a position where, objectively, his duty to give such advice conflicted with his duty to the defendant. The elements of bribery were thereby made out, and the claimant was entitled to rescission of its contracts with the defendant company and engineer and repayment of the sums it had paid thereunder.

42. The facts of *Panama Telegraph* suggest that, where the conflict and other elements of bribery are made out, it is irrelevant whether the payment to the agent by the third party is made in consideration of goods or services provided to the third party by the agent. There was no suggestion that the engineer's conduct could be excused on the ground that he provided the defendant company with engineering services in return for the secret payments it made him.

---

67 at p. 526

43. Similarly, in *Boston Deep Sea Fishing and Ice Company v Ansell,*[68] the managing director of the claimant company contracted to purchase fishing boats from a shipbuilding company and arranged to receive a lump sum payment and 1% commission on the value of payments to that company under the contract. The Court of Appeal described his actions as a "gross fraud" on the claimant company and refused to entertain any argument that he might be excused because he had also provided services to the shipbuilding company:

> *"There can be no question that an agent employed by a principal or master to do business with another, who, unknown to that principal or master, takes from that other a profit arising out of the business which he is employed to transact, is doing a wrongful act inconsistent with his duty towards his master and the continuation of confidence between them. He does the wrongful act, whether such profit be given to him in return for services which he actually performs towards the third party, or in return for services which he is supposed to perform, or for his supposed influence, or on any other ground at all. If it is a profit which arises out of the transaction, it belongs to his master, and he has no right to take it, or keep it, or bargain for it, unless his master knows it".*[69]

44. A number of further Victorian and modern cases could be cited for the proposition that bribery is made out where an undisclosed payment to an agent deprives the principal of the agent's impartial advice or services. *In Logicrose Ltd v Southend United Football Club*

[68] (1888) 39 Ch D 339

[69] per Bowen LJ at pp. 363-364

Limited[70], for instance, a director of the defendant company negotiated with the claimant for it to have a licence over land owned by the defendant. Unbeknown to his fellow directors, the director held shares in the defendant company as nominee for a third-party; and as a condition of granting the licence, he agreed with the claimant for it to pay £70,000 to an offshore company controlled by the third-party. When the defendant's board discovered these facts, it terminated the licence. The claimant brought a claim for damages and return of the £70,000, and the defendant counter-claimed for rescission of the licence and an account of the £70,000. The counter-claim succeeded for these reasons[71]:

> *"It is well established that a principal who discovers that his agent in a transaction has obtained or arranged to obtain a bribe or secret commission from the other party to the transaction is entitled, in addition to other remedies which may be open to him, to elect to rescind the transaction ab initio or, if it is too late to rescind, to bring it to an end for the future ... The remedy is not confined to cases where the agent has taken a bribe or secret commission in the strictest sense. It is available whenever, without his principal's knowledge and consent, the agent has put himself in a position where his interest and duty may conflict. A principal is entitled to the disinterested advice of his agent free from the potentially corrupting influence of an interest of his own. Any such private interest, whether actual or contemplated, which is not known and consented to by his principal, disqualifies him... It is immaterial whether the agent's mind has been affected or whether the principal has suffered any loss as a*

70 [1988] 1 WLR 1256

71 per Millett J at pp. 1260-1261

result... The principal, having been deprived by the other party to the transaction of the disinterested advice of his agent, is entitled to a further opportunity to consider whether it is in his interests to affirm it."

45. It follows from the above passage that, once a payment in circumstances giving rise to a conflict of interest has been made out, it is no defence for the agent to show that he was not in fact influenced by the payment when he advised his principal. The objective fact of the conflict is sufficient to make out liability for the purposes of the tort of bribery. Similarly, to make out liability there is no need for the principal to prove that the payment of the bribe caused him any actual loss (although of course he will need to prove the existence and extent of any loss at the remedy stage if he seeks damages rather than only rescission and/or an account of the bribe).

46. The requirements for the law of bribery to be engaged were considered at length by Christoper Clarke J in *Novoship (UK) Ltd v Mikhaylyuk*[72] ("*Novoship*"). The judge held that the:

> *"essential character of a bribe is that it is a secret payment or inducement that gives rise to a realistic prospect of a conflict between the agents personal interest and that of his principal. There is therefore no need for an actual (as distinct from potential) conflict of interest to exist at the time of the payment. A bribe encompasses not just a payment of money but the conferring of any advantage or benefit, and may be*

72 [2012] EWHC 3586 (Comm), at Paragraphs 104-110

an actual benefit or merely the promise of a benefit held out by the payer or an expectation of one".[73]

Nor does the payment need to be linked to a particular transaction: it is sufficient if the agent is tainted by the bribery at the time of the transaction between the payer of the bribe and payee's principal, and the principal is thereby deprived of the impartial advice of his agent. It follows that subsequent transactions may be tainted by payments linked to an earlier transaction between the parties, or by a payment not linked to any particular transaction, so long as the potential conflict of interest remains a real possibility. [74]

47. The judge described this as a strict approach, the underlying rationale for which is that a principal is entitled to be confident that an agent will act wholly in his interests.[75]

48. These paragraphs from Christopher Clarke J's judgment were approved by the Court of Appeal in *Eze v Conway*.[76] On the unusual facts of that case, however, the law of bribery was not engaged, as a self-described "acquisition agent" in relation to a very valuable property was not the purchaser's agent and did not owe him any fiduciary or similar duties. To the limited extent that he was an "agent" of the purchaser, he merely had a "ministerial" role in facilitating the transaction once the purchaser had decided in principle to buy the property.

---

73 at Paragraph 106

74 at Paragraph 109

75 at Paragraph 110

76 [2019] EWCA Civ 88

Need for "agency" or "fiduciary" relationship?

49. As mentioned above, the authorities on the law of bribery typically referred to "agents" and "principals" and/or "fiduciary duties" and "fiduciary relationships". This led to a lively debate as to whether an agency relationship and/or fiduciary duties were required for the law of bribery to be engaged. The payer or payee of a commission would typically contend that there was no such relationship and therefore the payment could not be a bribe.

50. This debate has for now been resolved for now by the Court of Appeal's decision in *Wood/Pengelly* and latterly was also considered in the *Johnson Wrench and Hopcraft*[77] case. The *Wood/Pengelly* conjoined appeals concerned mortgages which had been procured by brokers paid undisclosed commissions by the lenders despite the mortgage agreements containing the following term:

> '*We may receive fees from lenders with whom we place mortgages. Before we take out a mortgage, we will tell you the amount of the fee in writing. If the fee is less than £250, we will confirm that we will receive up to this amount. If the fee is £250 or more, we will tell you the exact amount.*'

51. The borrowers sought rescission of the mortgage agreements on the basis that the lenders had committed bribery by paying the

---

[77] N.B. permission to appeal has been granted by the Supreme Court in *Johnson, Wrench and Hopcraft* and the appeal is expected to be heard in April 2025. The Court of Appeal has asked for "*a definitive pronouncement to be made by the Supreme Court about the circumstances in which the payment of a commission by a third party to another person's agent or fiduciary will give rise to liability (whether as principal wrongdoer or an accessory) on the part of a payer*" (paragraph 178).

commissions without the disclosure promised in this term. The lenders resisted the claims on the basis that the brokers were not fiduciaries or agents in relation to the borrowers and therefore the law of bribery was not engaged.

52. After an extensive review of the authorities, David Richards LJ, giving the only substantive judgment, held that in such cases there was no need to engage in an extensive debate as to whether the recipient of the payment owed his principal fiduciary duties or not. Instead, he propounded a simpler test as follows:[78]

> *"To ask in cases of this kind whether there is a fiduciary relationship as a pre-condition for civil liability in respect of bribery or secret commissions is, in my judgment, an unnecessarily elaborate, and perhaps inaccurate, question. The question, I consider, is the altogether simpler one of whether the payee was under a duty to provide information, advice or recommendation on an impartial or disinterested basis. If the payee was under such a duty, the payment of bribes or secret commissions exposes the payer and the payee to the applicable civil remedies. No further enquiry as to the legal nature of their relationship is required."*

53. Similarly, in *Johnson, Wrench and Hopcraft,* all three claimants at County Court level argued that the car dealers owed them a duty to 'provide information, advice or recommendation on an impartial or disinterested basis'. The Court of Appeal held that there was a:

> *"disinterested duty which was sufficient to give rise to primary liability in the cases of Hopcraft and Wrench, which were secret commission cases. In all three cases there was also a*

78 at Paragraph 48

> *parallel fiduciary duty which was sufficient to found the claim for accessory liability in the Johnson case and would have been sufficient in Wrench had it been a partial disclosure case".*[79]

54. David Richards LJ's remarks at paragraph 48 of *Wood/Pengelly* (quoted above) concerned the liability of recipients or payers of secret commissions in the tort of bribery. Establishing a breach of fiduciary duty will often still be highly relevant where the claimant wishes to hold other defendants liable and/or seek the full range of equitable remedies. For this reason, David Richard LJ's remarks in the next paragraph should also be borne in mind[80]:

> *"This is not to say that, in the many cases in which a fiduciary relationship clearly exists, the remedies available cannot be analysed in terms of the consequences of a breach of fiduciary duty. If a fiduciary relationship exists, it is a breach of that duty for the fiduciary to accept a secret commission or the offer of a secret commission, and in such a case the payer or offeror will be procuring or assisting a breach of fiduciary duty. Both will be liable to a range of remedies: accounts of profits, compensation for loss and rescission of transactions."*

55. David Richards LJ also rejected any attempt to make liability for bribery depend on a strict application of the law of agency, which normally defines an "agent" as someone authorised to enter into legal relations with third parties on behalf of his principal[81]:

> *"I should add that in most of the cases the law on bribery and secret commissions is referred to as applying to payments to*

79 Paragraph 173(4) and Paragraphs 87 and 88

80 Paragraph 49

81 Paragraph 51

> *"agents", whether or not they are said to owe fiduciary duties. As will appear, I doubt whether the law on bribery is restricted to an "agent" properly so called, by which I mean a person authorised or ostensibly authorised to act on behalf of another. It is enough, in my view, that the person who is offered or paid a secret commission is, as Christopher Clarke J put it in Novoship (UK) Ltd v Mikhaylyuk [2012] EWHC 3586 (Comm) at [108], "someone with a role in the decision-making process in relation to the transaction in question e.g. as agent, or otherwise someone who is in a position to influence or affect the decision taken by the principal".*

56. The underlined words are a useful distillation of the circumstances in which the law of bribery will be engaged in relation to the recipient of a payment (or other economic benefit promised or conferred).

Johnson, Wrench and Hopcraft

57. In *Johnson, Wrench and Hopcraft,* the Court of Appeal considered three appeals on a conjoined basis. The facts of the cases were as follows:

(i) All three customers who were deemed to be financially unsophisticated customers purchased vehicles with the assistance of car finance.

(ii) In each case, the vehicle finance was arranged by a car dealer who worked with a panel of lenders and with whom the car dealer held an intermediary agreement for the payment of its commission[82]. The dealer then presented a finance option to each customer after gathering some financial information from the customer.

(iii) In the case of *Hopcraft,* there was no mention of any commission being payable in the car finance agreement. In *Wrench* the terms and conditions stated that a commission "may" be paid, in a sub-clause under the heading 'general'.

(iv) In *Johnson* the terms and conditions disclosed the possibility of a commission and this was stated in the 'suitability document' also.

(v) In all three cases, the commission structures at play provided the car dealer with the discretion to fix the interest "DCA".

(vi) In *Wrench* there was also a fixed commission structure in respect of a second agreement taken out by the customer as well as the DCA model in respect of the first one.

58. The Court of Appeal therefore determined the following key issues:

(i) Whether car dealers owe a disinterested and fiduciary duty to customers[83]?

---

82 The Court of Appeal referred to this as a "side arrangement" (Paragraph 4). In *Wrench* the schedule detailing the commission arrangement was fully redacted (Paragraph 27)

83 Paragraph 21(1)

(ii) Whether the possibility of the fact that a commission may be paid is enough to negate secrecy even where the borrower has neither read the statement nor been directed to read it[84]?

(iii) If there is a fiduciary duty in partial disclosure cases, what are the necessary ingredients to establish accessory liability on the part of the lender (accessory breach)?[85]

(iv) Whether the lender is liable for the repayment of commission?[86]

(v) Whether the payment of a secret commission will make the relationship between the creditor and debtor unfair[87].

59. The Court of Appeal recognised that there will be (i) those cases in which the fact of a commission payment was "fully secret" and those where there has been "partial disclosure"[88].

60. The Court of Appeal held that the duty owed by the car dealers in each case was a fiduciary duty which ran in tandem with a disinterested duty[89] .

---

[84] Paragraph 21(2)

[85] Paragraph 21(3)

[86] Paragraph 21(5)

[87] In respect of *Johnson* only (Paragraph 22)

[88] Paragraph 11

[89] Paragraph 91

61. The Court of Appeal found that in all three cases there was a conflict of interest and no informed consent by the consumers as to the payment of commission.[90]

62. The car dealers in *Wrench* and *Johnson* had regulatory obligations under CONC 4.5.3R.[91]

63. The lenders in the case of *Johnson* were "*liable in equity as an accessory to the broker's breach of fiduciary duty*", which the Court of Appeal found is a "*duty premised on credit brokers having a duty to be impartial in the first place*".[92]

64. In *Wrench* the Court of Appeal found that the Suitability Document presented to the customer contained "untruthful and misleading statements"[93] and was relevant to the unfairness claim.

65. The Court of Appeal confirmed that *Wood/Pengelly* is:

> "*an example of the orthodox application of settled principles pertaining to bribes and secret commissions*". [94]

66. Burying a statement in terms and conditions to the effect that a commission will or may be paid, which the consumer is unlikely to read, will not be enough to negate the secret nature of a commission payment[95].

---

[90] Paragraph 19

[91] Paragraph 96

[92] Paragraph 18

[93] Paragraph 48

[94] Paragraph 54

[95] See Paragraphs 37, 88 and 119

67. The lenders were held liable for the repayment of commissions to consumers[96].

68. In relation to the issue of what is required of a lender to bring a "partial disclosure" commission clause (referred to in comes previous cases as the "half-way house" scenario) to the attention of a consumer, the Court of Appeal stated that:

> *""Disclosure" in this context means taking reasonable steps to ensure that the fact actually comes to the attention of the consumer in a way which makes its significance apparent".*[97]

69. The above decision is currently subject to an appeal to the Supreme Court which is due to be heard at the beginning of April 2025 and has been referenced recently in the High Court case of *R (on the application of Clydesdale Financial Services Limited v Financial Ombudsman Service Limited (Arnold Clark Automobiles Limited, Jenna Lewis and the Financial Conduct Authority as interested parties).*[98]

Pre-action disclosure

70. In the context of pre-action disclosure in respect of what documents are required to be disclosed by lenders to a prospective claimant for a car finance claim, the only current authority on the point is the persuasive County Court decision of *Suleman & Others*

---

96 The CA held that it was not appropriate to award rescission in *Johnson* due to the passage of time since Mr Johnson sold his car (paragraph 142)

97 Paragraph 11

98 *[2024] EWHC 3237 (Admin)* at Paragraph 7

v Vauxhall, BMW and Black Horse[99], concerned an application for pre-action disclosure for commission documents. HHJ Khan[100] held that:

> "*once the customers know how much commission has been paid and how the commission has been calculated, they and their advisers can begin to investigate the merits and value of their respective claims*".

71. The FCA has also announced that in addition to firms maintaining adequate financial resources, it expects firms to deal with subject access requests appropriately and expects firms to:

> "*confirm, if a consumer asks, whether their agreement involved a DCA even if they haven't submitted a data subject access request*".[101]

---

99 *[2022] Burnley County Court (unreported)*. See also *Edwards & Others v Slater Gordon UK Limited [2022] EWHC 1091 QB*, per Richie.J. at paragraphs 224 which related to a claimant's appeal for a defendant to answer Part 18 questions in relation to alleged secret commissions received by a solicitor from the ATE insurer.

100 See Paragraph 133

101 See FCA's Dear CEO letter dated 12 April 2024

CHAPTER FOUR

CUSTOMER REDRESS: NON-LITIGIOUS ROUTES OF COMPLAINT

Regulatory bodies

72. The Motor Ombudsman ("MO") which was set up in November 2016 and is approved by the Government under the Alternative Dispute Resolution for Consumer Disputes (Competent Authorities and Information) Regulations 2015. It provides a dispute resolution process for complaints relating to the purchase of a vehicle rather than the finance to purchase such. Each accredited member is subject to its codes of practice. The Codes of Practice which are potentially relevant to the sale of vehicles are as follows:

    (i) The Vehicle Sales Code: This requires members to use transparent advertising methods, non-pressurised sales methods, provide accurate advice on warranty and finance products and provide a full vehicle handover with a full service history and MOT certificate.

    (ii) The Vehicle Warranty Products Code: This provides certain standards which members must comply with relating to advertising, point of sale obligations, clarity of information and complaints handling.

73. According to its annual report for 2021/22, used car sales complaints showed the highest volume of customer detriment. Its

key findings (as taken from the Motor Ombudsman's' Report for the period of 1 October 2021 to 30 September 2022[102]) made the following findings:

(i) *Consumer expectations are not always in line with the age or mileage of the vehicle. It is not always understood or appreciated that wear and tear items, such as brake pads, disks, clutches and exhaust systems may need replacing sooner after the sale than with a new vehicle, or that the vehicle may experience more unexpected defects. This can be exacerbated where this occurs soon after purchase or leads to a higher than anticipated bill with consumers feeling that they are entitled to some kind of remedy – even if the issue is age or mileage-related, and not covered by consumer rights legislation.*

(ii) *Equally, businesses selling used vehicles may be more hesitant to support repair costs as they do not believe they are liable for problems that arise. They may also rely on a warranty to cover the costs of repair, but the terms of a warranty may be limited, and this can lead to confusion over a consumer's rights under the Consumer Rights Act 2015 and other legislation, as well as their rights under the warranty. There may be instances in which a fault on a used car gives rise to an entitlement under consumer law, and it is important for businesses to be able to distinguish when this is the case as opposed to asserting "the price has been lowered to reflect its condition".*

102 https://www.themotorombudsman.org/wp-content/uploads/2016/12/THE-MOTOR-OMBUDSMAN-ANNUAL-REPORT-2021.pdf

(iii) *There can also be issues with understanding approved used car schemes, as the terms and conditions as well as what is covered under the scheme varies from business to business. It may also be the case that a vehicle sold under the approved used scheme, does not meet the requirements of the scheme – for example, it does not have a full-service history. Consumers have a reasonably higher expectation of vehicles sold under approved used schemes and, therefore feel more aggrieved when the vehicle falls below the desired standard. Businesses need to ensure they only market vehicles under a scheme if they meet the eligibility requirements and in managing consumer expectations of quality and durability.*

74. As regards the sale of electric vehicles, the MO reported that over 1,500 complaints had been submitted for the first 9 months of 2024, nearly double the volume of the previous year.[103]

75. Additionally the Financial Ombudsman Service ("FOS") deal with complaints against lenders and authorised car dealers in respect of credit agreements[104]. The High Court case of *R (on the application of Clydesdale Financial Services Limited v Financial Ombudsman Service Limited (Arnold Clark Automobiles Limited, Jenna Lewis and the Financial Conduct Authority as interested parties),*[105] involved a complaint made by a Ms Lewis in respect of

[103] https://www.themotorombudsman.org/useful-information/automotive-views/ev-disputes-brought-by-consumers-to-tmo-in-q3-2024

[104] See DISP App 5.1.1 to 5.3.2 and DISP, DISP 1.1.2, DISP 3.6.1, CONRED 5.1 and s.229 of FSMA 2000

[105] *[2024] EWHC 3237 (Admin)* at Paragraph 7

commission arrangements in respect of a conditional sale agreement not being disclosed to her. In a judicial review claim brought by Clydesdale Financial Services Limited, the High Court upheld the decision made by FOS in respect of the award it recommended to Miss L against Clydesdale Financial Services Limited which included the following grounds:

(i) Whether the Ombudsman misinterpreted the relevant provisions of the FCA Handbook governing the conduct of regulated persons and bodies in the financial services industry;[106]

(ii) whether the Ombudsman was right to conclude that the commission arrangements between Clydesdale and the car dealer, Arnold Clark should have been disclosed or more fully disclosed to Ms Lewis;[107]

(iii) whether the Ombudsman erred in law, disregarded relevant considerations or reached an irrational conclusion when deciding to make a monetary award in favour of Ms Lewis;[108]

76. The High Court[109] dismissed all three grounds of appeal brought by the lender, finding that the FOS interpreted FCA regulatory rules and the Consumer Credit Act 1974 (CCA 1974) correctly.

---

106 See Paragraph 9 of the judgment

107 See Paragraph 9 of the judgment

108 See Paragraph 9 of the judgment

109 Permission to appeal has been granted to the Court of Appeal in this case and the decision may therefore be subject to change

77. Complaints in relation to discretionary commission arrangements have been extended to 4 December 2025 by virtue of a change to the FCA's Dispute Resolutions Complaints Rules (DISP). Under the new rules, the FCA has imposed a 37-week suspension to the 8-week time limit for motor finance firms to provide a final response to complaints in relation to DCAs. At the same time, the FCA extended the time limit for complainants to refer DCA complaints to firms from 6 months to 15 months. These new DISP Rules apply to both lenders and car dealers in the motor finance market[110].

---

[110] See DISP App 5.1.1 to 5.3.2

CHAPTER FIVE

UNFAIR RELATIONSHIP CLAIMS

78. A court can award a remedy to a consumer debtor if it concludes that the relationship between the consumer and the lender (creditor) is (or was) 'unfair'. The court's powers are governed by sections 140A-C of the Consumer Credit Act 1974 ('the Act').

What amounts to *unfairness*?

79. There is no statutory definition of unfairness. There are, however, specific circumstances in which a court can go on to make an award; section 140A of the Act provides that:

(1) The court may make an order under section 140B in connection with a credit agreement if it determines that the relationship between the creditor and the debtor arising out of the agreement (or the agreement taken with any related agreement) is unfair to the debtor because of one or more of the following—

(a) any of the terms of the agreement or of any related agreement;

(b) the way in which the creditor has exercised or enforced any of his rights under the agreement or any related agreement;

(c) any other thing done (or not done) by, or on behalf of, the creditor (either before or after the making of the agreement or any related agreement).

(emphasis added)

80. If one of those categories applies, the court will move on to consider whether to grant a remedy. The court's discretion is in no way constrained; section 140A(2) of the Act states that:

> *(2) In deciding whether to make a determination under this section the court shall have regard to all matters it thinks relevant (including matters relating to the creditor and matters relating to the debtor).*

81. In other words, the court will stand back and undertake a sense-check before making an award of compensation or otherwise. Section 140A is therefore a broad church which aims to achieve fairness.

82. The Act clearly gives rise to consideration of the whole relationship between the lender and the consumer, and therefore concerns *things done (or not done)* by the lender. The court's consideration is not, however, confined to that of the lender; car dealers and other brokers play a pivotal, customer-facing role in arranging car finance agreements and so their conduct, insofar as they act as agents of the lender, will be scrutinised by the court. Indeed, section 140A(3) provides that:

> *(3) For the purposes of this section the court shall (except to the extent that it is not appropriate to do so) treat anything done (or not done) by, or on behalf of, or in relation to, an associate or a former associate of the*

creditor as if done (or not done) by, or on behalf of, or in relation to, the creditor.

83. Section 140A(4) of the Act enables a court to to make a determination 'notwithstanding that the relationship may have ended' (see more in the chapter on Limitation).

Remedies

84. The court has wide powers when it comes to remedies. Section 140B(1) sets out the orders which the court may make:

(1) An order under this section in connection with a credit agreement may do one or more of the following—]

(a) require the creditor, or any associate or former associate of his, to repay (in whole or in part) any sum paid by the debtor or by a surety by virtue of the agreement or any related agreement (whether paid to the creditor, the associate or the former associate or to any other person);

(b) require the creditor, or any associate or former associate of his, to do or not to do (or to cease doing) anything specified in the order in connection with the agreement or any related agreement;

(c) reduce or discharge any sum payable by the debtor or by a surety by virtue of the agreement or any related agreement;

(d) direct the return to a surety of any property provided by him for the purposes of a security;

(e) *otherwise set aside (in whole or in part) any duty imposed on the debtor or on a surety by virtue of the agreement or any related agreement;*

(f) *alter the terms of the agreement or of any related agreement;*

(g) *direct accounts to be taken, or (in Scotland) an accounting to be made, between any persons.*

85. It is important to remember that any remedy is intended to address the unfairness between the parties. The court will usually address any unfairness by ordering the lender to pay a sum of money to the consumer. The power to order repayment of *any sum paid by the debtor* is undoubtedly a flexible remedy. In the author's experience, the courts are reluctant to make a money order beyond the equivalent of the sum of commission plus interest thereon. The rationale for such an approach is to recognise that the consumer needed and therefore benefitted from the credit advanced by the Lender.

86. In a case involving a discretionary commission arrangement ("DCA") (i.e. a difference-in-charges or other DCA model), the court might also award the difference between a fair sum of interest and the interest in fact charged at the car dealer's discretion rather than ordering a simple return of the commission.

Burdens of proof

87. The consumer carries the burden of proving the factual basis for the claim. For example, if a term of the agreement is alleged to be unfair, then there should be a clear, particularised pleading as why the term is or was unfair. Further, the claimant's particulars of

claim ought to set out the things *done or not done* by the lender and the dealer/broker.

88. Once a claimant has alleged unfairness, the burden rests upon the lender to prove that the relationship was not unfair. Indeed, section 140B(9) of the Act says:

> *If in any such proceedings the debtor or a surety alleges that a relationship between the creditor and the debtor is unfair to the debtor, it is for the creditor to prove to the contrary.*

Legal authorities

89. There are limited authorities on the application of section 140 of the Act. That is perhaps unsurprising given its broad application.

90. The courts' approach to *unfairness* in the context of hidden commissions developed in the Payment Protection Insurance (PPI) landscape.

91. In *Harrison v Black Horse Limited*[111], PPI was sold to the claimant during the negotiation of a loan. Mr and Mrs Harrison argued that the relationship was unfair because there was a failure to disclose the fact that 87% of the cost of the PPI was in fact a commission to the insurer. Notwithstanding the size of the commission, the Court of Appeal rejected Mr and Mrs Harrison's arguments that the relationship was unfair because there was no regulatory requirement in either the ICOB Rules or Insurance Mediation Directive for the commission to be disclosed. The court therefore

[111] [2011] EWCA Civ 2011

placed importance on the standards imposed by the regulators when considering the question of unfairness.

92. The UK Supreme Court then came to consider the issue of unfairness in *Plevin v Paragon Personal Finance Limited*[112]. In a unanimous decision of the court, Lord Sumption opined that *Harrison* was wrongly decided:

> *17. It follows that the question whether the debtor-creditor relationship is fair cannot be the same as the question whether the creditor has complied with the ICOB rules, and the facts which may be relevant to answer it are manifestly different. An altogether wider range of considerations may be relevant to the fairness of the relationship, most of which would not be relevant to the application of the rules. They include the characteristics of the borrower, her sophistication or vulnerability, the facts which she could reasonably be expected to know or assume, the range of choices available to her, and the degree to which the creditor was or should have been aware of these matters.*

93. Mrs Plevin took out a personal loan which was repayable in instalments over ten years. She also purchased PPI for five years. The PPI premium was £5,780, which was payable at the outset and added to the loan. 71.8% of the premium was taken in commission and split between the lender and the broker. The broker provided Mrs Plevin with a Financial Industry Standards Association guide which confirmed that "*commission is paid by the lending company*". She was not, however, told the amount of the commission or the identity of the recipients.

112 [2014] UKSC 61

94. In dismissing Paragon's appeal, Lord Sumption considered the issues of (i) the non-disclosure of the commissions, and (ii) the failure to assess the suitability of PPI insurance for Mrs Plevin's needs.

95. As to the first issue, Lord Sumption said this:

> *18. I turn therefore to the question whether the non-disclosure of the commissions payable out of Mrs Plevin's PPI premium made her relationship with Paragon unfair. In my opinion, it did. A sufficiently extreme inequality of knowledge and understanding is a classic source of unfairness in any relationship between a creditor and a non-commercial debtor. It is a question of degree. Mrs Plevin must be taken to have known that some commission would be payable to intermediaries out of the premium before it reached the insurer. The fact was stated in the FISA borrowers' guide and, given that she was not paying LLP for their services, there was no other way that they could have been remunerated. But at some point commissions may become so large that the relationship cannot be regarded as fair if the customer is kept in ignorance. At what point is difficult to say, but wherever the tipping point may lie the commissions paid in this case are a long way beyond it. Mrs Plevin's evidence, as recorded by the Recorder, was that if she had known that 71.8% of the premium would be paid out in commissions, she would have "certainly questioned this." I do not find that evidence surprising. The information was of critical relevance. Of course, had she shopped around, she would not necessarily have got better terms. As the Competition Commission's report suggests, this was not a competitive market. But Mrs Plevin did not have to*

> *take PPI at all. Any reasonable person in her position who was told that more than two thirds of the premium was going to intermediaries, would be bound to question whether the insurance represented value for money, and whether it was a sensible transaction to enter into. The fact that she was left in ignorance in my opinion made the relationship unfair.*

96. Mrs Plevin did not succeed on the second issue although this did not materially affect the outcome of her claim. The court found that there was no agency between the broker and the lender. The court did not therefore attach the broker's conduct to the lender for the purposes of section 140A(3) of the Act.

Partial disclosure cases (aka half-secret commissions)

97. Where secrecy has not been negated, it is difficult to see why a court would not conclude that the relationship was unfair.

But, what about partial-disclosure cases?

98. *Plevin* was a case in which secrecy was negated but the relationship was nevertheless held to have been unfair.

99. Similarly, in Nelmes v NRAM Plc[113], Christopher Clarke LJ said:

> *The claim against NR in the present action is not a claim that it should account for the commission or for rescission of the credit agreement, but that relief should be given because of the unfair nature of the relationship. That claim raises different,*

[113] [2016] EWCA Civ 491

and broader, considerations. I am, however, quite satisfied that in this respect the relationship between NR, the creditor, and Mr Nelmes, the debtor, arising out of the loan agreements was unfair on account of the combination of the following: (i) the term of the credit agreement that Mr Nelmes should pay NR an arrangement fee; (ii) the related agreement that NR should pay commission of half that amount to Mr Nelmes' broker; (iii) the payment of that commission; and (iv) the failure of NR to tell Nelmes about the payment. A relationship between lender and borrower which involves such a payment deprives the borrower of the disinterested advice of his broker and is, for that reason, unfair.

Unfair relationships in car finance cases

100. In car finance claims, lenders often argue that, unlike in Mrs Plevin's case, the claimant did not directly pay for the commission. That may be so where the commission was by way of a fixed sum, although there is arguably an indirect cost in all such cases. DCAs, on the other hand, ordinarily come at a price to the consumer: the higher the interest rate, the greater the cost of credit to the consumer.

101. Lenders also tend to argue that the commission sum is significantly less than the cost of the interest charged (the 'cost of credit') and so does not reach the tipping point described by Lord Sumption. Whilst a trial judge might be persuaded that the cost of credit is not wholly out of proportion with the cost of credit, commissions flowing from car finance agreements are

unlikely to be viewed as insignificant by most consumers[114]. They also arguably differ from PPI claims in that the commission relates to a loan used to purchase an asset rather than an add-on insurance product.

No 'but-for' causation test

102. Whilst a claimant does not have to prove that disclosure of the size of the commission, or indeed the type of commission model, would have *caused* them to act differently — indeed, the court need only be satisfied that the source of unfairness would have been removed[115] — a claimant will at least be expected to demonstrate that he would have questioned the commission or the value of the credit agreement. Notwithstanding that *but-for* causation does not have to be established, the court can take account of evidence by a claimant that he would not have proceeded to enter the agreement had he known the size of the commission.

Johnson v FirstRand Bank Limited (London Branch) t/a Motonovo Finance[116]

103. The judgment of the Court of Appeal provides helpful guidance as to the application of section 140 of the Act in the context of car finance claims.

---

114 In *Jones v BMW Financial Services Limited (2023, unreported)*, HHJ Carter determined that the relationship was unfair in circumstances in which a 'half-secret commission' of £300 was paid by a Lender to a dealer in respect of a loan of £45,534.13 (with an APR at 5.4%).

115 See *Plevin*, at paragraph 20

116 [2024] EWCA Civ 1282

104. Mr Johnson obtained a Suzuki motor car by way of a loan provided by Motonovo Finance (the lender). The loan was proposed and arranged by the car dealer.

105. The dealer was paid a commission of £1,650.95 which represented almost 70% of the cost of credit, or 25.8% of the total sum advanced. The type of commission model is set out at paragraph 50 of the judgment: the broker had a discretion to set interest rates between a range of 8% to 13%. Interest was charged at a flat rate of 8%, There was, however, a further commission at 25% of the sum advanced. The sum of commission was therefore determined solely by reference to the sum advanced.

106. The lender's terms and conditions disclosed the possibility that a commission would be paid to the dealer, and such possibility was also referred to in the 'Suitability Document' created and provided by the dealer. Mr Johnson conceded that the fact of the commission arrangement was not fully secret, no doubt because of those written disclosures.

107. In addition to arguing that the dealer, assisted by the lender, breached its fiduciary and disinterested duties to him, Mr Johnson alleged that his relationship with the lender was unfair.

108. In the course of proceedings, the lender disclosed its commercial agreement with the dealer which revealed that the dealer was not only obliged to give the lender first refusal in respect of finance provided to its customers but was also also required to use reasonable endeavours to introduce its customers to the lender.

109. An extract from Mr Johnson's witness statement is set out at paragraph 43 of the *Johnson* judgment. His statement confirmed that he had "*absolutely no idea that commission was commonly*

paid in this industry and was very surprised to learn exactly how much commission was paid under my agreement". The lender produced no evidence to prove that Mr Johnson was told otherwise.

110. The court placed significant weight on concerns arising from the Suitability Document, as can be seen in the following damning passage:

> *48. Although it made reference to the possible payment of a commission, and made it clear that the broker was not going to search the whole market, there were a number of materially untruthful and misleading statements in the Suitability Document (see [153] to [156] below). In consequence the document created the false impression that the Trade Centre Wales were exercising their judgement in selecting a finance provider which "may be most appropriate" for the customer's needs from a panel of 22 lenders, when in fact there was an undisclosed obligation which tied the broker into giving FirstRand first refusal in every case. The misleading nature of the Suitability Document is a matter which is of some significance when we come to consider the claim by Mr Johnson under the 1974 Act.*

111. In contrast to the finding in *Plevin,* the dealer *was* considered to be acting as the lender's agent[117]. As such, the dealer's conduct was relevant when considering *things done (or not done)* for the purposes of section 140A(3) of the Act.

---

[117] Accordingly, the court was satisfied that section 56 of the Act (see paragraphs 145 and 160)

112. The court held that the Suitability Document was "untruthful" because the agreement with the lender was not the most suitable for Mr Johnson's requirements.

113. There was also criticism of the commercial agreement between the lender and the dealer. The lender placed no obligation on the dealer to disclose its contractual tie-in with the lender. The court concluded that a reasonable reader would deduce from the Suitability Document that the dealer would select a lender from a select panel which was most suitable to Mr Johnson's needs. Rather, the dealer proposed only the lender and plainly benefitted from doing so.

114. On the facts of the case, the court concluded that the relationship was unfair:

> *In fact, the reality was that the Trade Centre Wales made no attempt to be impartial between different lenders in the interests of the consumer. All the business was offered to FirstRand. The dealer gave the customer the Suitability Document which actively concealed the reality. The dealer offered no service to Mr Johnson as a broker at all except to introduce him to one lender to whom it was tied by Clause 2.1 of the Dealer Terms of Business and from whom it took a lavish commission. The existence of the relationship between lender and dealer in this case was such as to require honest and accurate disclosure so that the customer could decide whether he wanted to buy a car with finance obtained through a dealer/credit broker who would conduct at least*

> *some review of what the credit market, or a panel of lenders within it, might offer him*[118].

115. The fact that the commission was 25% of the sum advanced was a key fact, as was the fact that Mr Johnson borrowed and paid the dealer more than the car was worth (the cash price itself was considerably more than the Glass's Guide retail price).

116. More generally, the court pronounced at paragraph 171 that:

> *Ordinarily, this court would hesitate to reach conclusions on issues which have not been fully dealt with either at trial or on first appeal, but this kind of case requires rather less caution in that regard than others. The oral evidence of the appellant is, so far as it goes, very straightforward and uncontradicted. The relevant discussions took place many years before the trial (as will often be the case) and it is inevitable that the primary focus will be on the documents, including those which were available to Mr Johnson at the time of the transaction and those which reveal the arrangements between the lender and the broker.*

117. The court made its own determination on remedy without hearing submissions: the commission of £1,650 was ordered to be repaid to Mr Johnson together with the interest he paid on it, plus interest thereon at a commercial rate from the date of the agreement to the date of judgment.

118 Paragraph 166

Conclusion

118. The following practical points arise in unfair relationship claims:

- The Particulars of claim should set out all facts which are relevant to the case, by reference to the categories at section 140A(1) of the Act, as well as any other factors which go to the question of fairness between the parties.
- The size of the commission is likely to be a highly relevant fact, if not determinative of the question of fairness.
- The question of disclosure, the claimant's level of sophistication, and whether the claimant's informed consent to the commission was secured are further, important considerations.
- The conduct of both the lender and the dealer (as the lender's agent) is relevant to the issue of fairness and consideration of all matters relevant to the claimant and the lender.
- All documents, including the agreement and its terms and conditions, the '*suitability*' document and other pre-contractual documents, and the commercial agreement (often referred to as a Rates and Terms document) should be scrutinised.
- The question of compliance with regulatory rules and guidance (within the FCA's Consumer Credit Sourcebook (CONC)) is also relevant.

CHAPTER SIX

LIMITATION

119. This chapter considers the time limits by which (i) unfair relationship claims, and (ii) undisclosed commission claims should be brought.

120. The Limitation Act 1980 ("the Act) sets the primary time limits by which actions should be commenced in court.

Unfair relationship claims

121. Section 9(1) of the Act provides that:

> *An action to recover any sum recoverable by virtue of any enactment shall not be brought after the expiration of six years from the date on which the cause of action accrued.*

Undisclosed/Secret commission claims

122. Section 5 of the Act provides that:

> *An action founded on simple contract shall not be brought after the expiration of six years from the date on which the cause of action accrued.*

123. A claim for recovery of secret commissions is a claim for monies had and received. Section 5 of the Act therefore applies. If, on the other hand, the court were to view the claim as one for equitable compensation, the section 5 limitation period

nevertheless applies by analogy (by operation of section 36 of the Act).

When does the cause of action accrue and the six-year limitation period therefore commence?

Unfair relationship claims

124. It is now clear from *Smith and another v Royal Bank of Scotland Plc*[119] that the cause of action does not accrue for limitation purposes until the relationship ceases to be unfair.[120]

125. Ms Smith was sold Payment Protection Insurance by RBS when she was issued with a credit card. RBS did not disclose that most of the PPI premium was retained by RBS as commission rather than being paid to the insurer. Ms Smith first became aware that RBS had received commission in 2018 when RBS offered a sum of money which was said to be the sum of commission in excess of 50% of the sum she had paid for PPI. By the time the case reached the UK Supreme Court, the exact size of the commission had not been disclosed by RBS.

126. The Supreme Court noted that where a relationship is continuing, the question to be decided is not whether the relationship *was* unfair (i.e. at the time when the agreement was entered into or at some other time in the past); rather, the court would be determining whether the continuing relationship *is* unfair. In that case, the limitation clock would not have even started to tick.

---

119 [2023] UKSC 34

120 The decision is consistent with the High Court's reasoning in *Patel v Patel [2009] EWHC 3264 (QB)*

127. Where, on the other hand, the relationship has ended, the wording in section 140A(4) of the Consumer Credit Act 1974 means that the cause of action accrues on the day when the relationship ended.

128. Accordingly, in the case of a car finance agreement, if (by way of example) the loan was discharged/settled on 31 December 2021, the claim would have to be commenced within 6 years of that date, i.e. by 31 December 2027.

Undisclosed/Secret commission claims

129. A different starting point applies to equitable or common law 'secret commission' claims.

130. In the context of a car finance agreement, given that such a claim concerns a breach of duty by the dealer (assisted by the lender) in receiving a commission from the lender, the cause of action accrues at the time when the commission is paid. Accordingly, a claim would have to be commenced at court within 6 years of the date of payment.

But what is the position if the six-year time limit has passed? Can a claim still be brought?

131. Possibly, yes. There are circumstances in which the court can postpone the six-year time limit. Section 32 of the Act provides that:

> (1) … where in the case of any action for which a period of limitation is prescribed by this Act, either—
>
> (a) the action is based upon the fraud of the defendant; or

> (b) any fact relevant to the plaintiff's right of action has been deliberately concealed from him by the defendant; or
>
> (c) the action is for relief from the consequences of a mistake;
>
> the period of limitation shall not begin to run until the plaintiff has discovered the fraud, concealment or mistake(as the case may be) or could with reasonable diligence have discovered it.
>
> (2) For the purposes of subsection (1) above, deliberate commission of a breach of duty in circumstances in which it is unlikely to be discovered for some time amounts to deliberate concealment of the facts involved in that breach of duty.

132. In *Canada Square Operations Ltd v Potter*[121], Mrs Potter relied on the section 32(1)(b) and 32(2) *deliberate concealment* provisions in her section 140A *unfair relationship* claim. Mrs Potter entered into a credit agreement with the lender in 2006, which consisted of a cash loan of £16,953.00 and a payment protection insurance premium of £3,834.24. Over 95% of the premium was paid to the lender for selling the PPI policy. Mrs Potter was not told about the commission and the loan agreement with the lender ended in March 2010.

133. In November 2018, Mrs Potter became aware of the commission on taking legal advice. She commenced court proceedings a month later, in December 2018. Her case

[121] [2021] EWCA Civ 339

proceeded to trial and she relied upon the section 32 deliberate concealment provisions in response to the lender's limitation defence. The trial judge found that those provisions did apply and that the limitation period did not begin to run until November 2018. Both the High Court and the Court of Appeal dismissed the lender's appeal and the case ultimately came before the Supreme Court.

134. There were 2 issues before the Supreme Court:

(i) Did the lender conceal a fact relevant to Mrs Potter's claim within the meaning of section 32(1)(b) of the Act?

(ii) Did the lender's conduct amount to a deliberate commission of a breach of duty for the purposes of section 32(2) of the Act?

135. On the first issue, the court held that a fact can be concealed either by taking active steps to conceal it or by failing to disclose it; either way, a claimant will need to establish that the defendant <u>intended</u> to do either of those things. It is not enough to show that the defendant *recklessly* concealed the relevant fact(s). In Mrs Potter's case, the relevant facts which Mrs Potter needed to know in order to plead her case were both the *existence* and the *amount* of commission. The court found that the lender had *deliberately concealed* those facts because it had consciously decided not to disclose them to Mrs Potter. Further, and finally, there was no suggestion that Mrs Potter could have discovered the concealment earlier than November 2018 when she took legal advice.

136. As to the second issue, the court confirmed that a claimant who seeks to rely on section 32(2) of the Act needs to prove that a

defendant knew it was committing a breach of duty or that it intended to do so. The court rejected the contention that '*reckless*' conduct (i.e. unreasonably proceeding in the face of known risks) amounted to a deliberate commission of a breach of duty. On the facts of the Mrs Potter's case, it could not be said that the lender knew or intended that the relationship was unfair because of any failure to disclose the fact and amount of commission.

137. The lender's appeal therefore failed before the Supreme Court on the first issue and Mrs Potter's claim ultimately succeeded.

Deliberate concealment in car finance claims

138. At the time of writing, there is no authoritative decision as to the application of section 32 in the context of a car finance agreement.

139. Consumers of car finance have come to explore potential claims because of the rapidly growing marketing and media coverage in this area of financial mis-selling.

140. In the author's experience, limitation arguments tend to go as follows:

141. Claimants argue that they did not know the following facts in the 6 years preceding the commencement of their claim: (i) that a commission had, in fact, been paid (and that it is not enough for a lender to argue that the *possibility* of commission was disclosed in pre-contractual documentation), and (ii) the amount of the commission in fact paid. It is not uncommon for those facts to be withheld until a claim is pursued. Disclosure of the *amount* of commission might only come by way of a defence

or witness evidence; indeed, claimants argue that they would not have been told about the fact or amount of commission even if they had asked.

142. Defendants often counter-argue that a claimant need not know every fact in order to plead a claim[122], pointing to the fact that (i) the claimant has been able to plead a case without knowing the facts allegedly concealed and (ii) the claimant was aware of the *possibility* of commission from the pre-contractual or other disclosure documentation and could have asked for confirmation of the amount of commission if they had any concerns about commission. In other words, such action by the claimant would have amounted to reasonable diligence for the purposes of section 32(1)(b) of the Act.

143. Lenders have also tended to plead that there is or was no regulatory obligation on a dealer/broker to disclose the *amount* of commission because CONC rule 4.5.3 only requires the broker to disclose the existence and nature of commission and that, having done so through the agreement, pre-contractual or other disclosure documentation, the onus to seek confirmation of the amount of commission passed to the claimant by virtue of CONC rule 4.5.4. The relevance of the CONC rules in this context is, for now, unclear. In *Canada Square,* the Supreme Court said that a claimant does not need to establish that a defendant was under a legal, moral or social duty to disclose a fact. Rather, the central question for the court under section 32(1)(b) is whether the defendant intended to keep the claimant in the dark about the fact in question (i.e. the existence or

---

[122] Reliance is often placed on *Gemalto Holdings BV and Others v Infineon Technologies AG and Others [2022] EWCA Civ 782*

amount of the commission), such that the claimant could not bring the claim within the six-year time limit.

144. The issue of limitation did not fall for the Court of Appeal's consideration in the conjoined appeals in *Johnson v FirstRand Bank Ltd t/a Motonovo Finance*[123], and so there was no need for the court to determine whether there had been deliberate concealment and which facts which would be relevant to that question. It is, however, notable that in the case of *Wrench* (a fully secret commission case), the court referred to a general reference to the possibility of a commission payment as having been "a *carefully concealed* sub-clause of their standard terms [where there was] an attempt to divert attention from it in the manner which occurred here"[124]. It is therefore, perhaps, apparent that the court would have had no difficulty in applying section 32.

Conclusion

145. Limitation defences therefore give rise to the following considerations:

- What is the cause of action for the purposes of the primary limitation period, and has that primary limitation period expired?
- When did the relationship end? The time limit for the purposes of the section 140A unfair relationship claim will

[123] [2024] EWCA Civ 1282

[124] See paragraph 119

begin to run from the end of the relationship (*Smith v RBS*).

- When was the commission paid? The exact date is not likely to be known but is likely to have been on or soon after the finance agreement was entered into.

- If the six-year time limit has expired (in respect of any cause of action), has there been a deliberate concealment of a relevant fact which the claimant could not discover with reasonable diligence?

- In cases where secrecy has not been negated, section 32 is likely to apply.

- In cases where secrecy has been negated, the claimant will need to establish that there has been deliberate concealment and the parties will need to pay careful consideration to the facts relevant the cause of action, including the conduct of the dealer, and the commercial agreement between the dealer and lender.

MORE BOOKS BY LAW BRIEF PUBLISHING

A selection of our other titles available now:-

'The Electronic Communications Code: A Practical Guide – Second Edition' by Kerry Bretherton KC, James Castle, Mark Loveday
'A Practical Guide to the Independent School Standards – September 2023 Edition' by Sarah McKimm
'A Practical Guide to Estate Administration and Crypto Assets' by Richard Marshall
'A Practical Guide to Parental Alienation in Private and Public Law Children Cases' by Sam King QC & Frankie Shama
'Contested Heritage – Removing Art from Land and Historic Buildings' by Richard Harwood QC, Catherine Dobson, David Sawtell
'The Limits of Separate Legal Personality: When Those Running a Company Can Be Held Personally Liable for Losses Caused to Third Parties Outside of the Company' by Dr Mike Wilkinson
'A Practical Guide to Transgender Law' by Robin Moira White & Nicola Newbegin
'A Practical Guide to 'Stranded Spouses' in Family Law' by Mani Singh Basi
'A Practical Guide to Residential Freehold Conveyancing' by Lorraine Richardson
'A Practical Guide to Pensions on Divorce for Lawyers' by Bryan Scant
'A Practical Guide to Challenging Sham Marriage Allegations in Immigration Law' by Priya Solanki
'A Practical Guide to Digital Communications Evidence in Criminal Law' by Sam Willis
'A Practical Guide to Legal Rights in Scotland' by Sarah-Jane Macdonald
'A Practical Guide to New Build Conveyancing' by Paul Sams & Rebecca East
'A Practical Guide to Inherited Wealth on Divorce' by Hayley Trim
'A Practical Guide to Practice Direction 12J and Domestic Abuse in Private Law Children Proceedings' by Rebecca Cross & Malvika Jaganmohan
'A Practical Guide to Confiscation and Restraint' by Narita Bahra QC, John Carl Townsend, David Winch
'A Practical Guide to the Law of Forests in Scotland' by Philip Buchan
'A Practical Guide to Health and Medical Cases in Immigration Law' by Rebecca Chapman & Miranda Butler
'A Practical Guide to Bad Character Evidence for Criminal Practitioners by Aparna Rao
'A Practical Guide to Extradition Law post-Brexit' by Myles Grandison et al
'A Practical Guide to Hoarding and Mental Health for Housing Lawyers' by Rachel Coyle

'Stephens on Contractual Indemnities' by Richard Stephens
'A Practical Guide to the EU Succession Regulation' by Richard Frimston
'A Practical Guide to Solicitor and Client Costs – Second Edition' by Robin Dunne
'Constructive Dismissal – Practice Pointers and Principles' by Benjimin Burgher
'A Practical Guide to Religion and Belief Discrimination Claims in the Workplace' by Kashif Ali
'A Practical Guide to the Law of Medical Treatment Decisions' by Ben Troke
'Fundamental Dishonesty and QOCS in Personal Injury Proceedings: Law and Practice' by Jake Rowley
'A Practical Guide to the Law in Relation to School Exclusions' by Charlotte Hadfield & Alice de Coverley
'A Practical Guide to Divorce for the Silver Separators' by Karin Walker
'The Right to be Forgotten – The Law and Practical Issues' by Melissa Stock
'A Practical Guide to Planning Law and Rights of Way in National Parks, the Broads and AONBs' by James Maurici QC, James Neill et al
'A Practical Guide to Election Law' by Tom Tabori
'A Practical Guide to the Law in Relation to Surrogacy' by Andrew Powell
'A Practical Guide to Claims Arising from Fatal Accidents – Second Edition' by James Patience
'A Practical Guide to Asbestos Claims' by Jonathan Owen & Gareth McAloon
'A Practical Guide to Stamp Duty Land Tax in England and Northern Ireland' by Suzanne O'Hara
'A Practical Guide to the Law of Farming Partnerships' by Philip Whitcomb
'A Practical Guide to the Law of Unlawful Eviction and Harassment – Second Edition' by Stephanie Lovegrove
'A Practical Guide to Costs in Personal Injury Claims – Second Edition' by Matthew Hoe
'A Practical Guide to the General Data Protection Regulation (GDPR) – Second Edition' by Keith Markham
'A Practical Guide to Working with Litigants in Person and McKenzie Friends in Family Cases' by Stuart Barlow
'Protecting Unregistered Brands: A Practical Guide to the Law of Passing Off' by Lorna Brazell
'A Practical Guide to Secondary Liability and Joint Enterprise Post-Jogee' by Joanne Cecil & James Mehigan

'A Practical Guide to the Pre-Action RTA Claims Protocol for Personal Injury Lawyers' by Antonia Ford
'A Practical Guide to Neighbour Disputes and the Law' by Alexander Walsh
'A Practical Guide to Coercive Control for Legal Practitioners and Victims' by Rachel Horman
'A Practical Guide to the Law of Driverless Cars – Second Edition'
by Alex Glassbrook, Emma Northey & Scarlett Milligan
'A Practical Guide to TOLATA Claims' by Greg Williams
'A Practical Guide to Elderly Law – Second Edition' by Justin Patten
'A Practical Guide to Responding to Housing Disrepair and Unfitness Claims' by Iain Wightwick
'A Practical Guide to the Law of Bullying and Harassment in the Workplace' by Philip Hyland
'How to Be a Freelance Solicitor: A Practical Guide to the SRA-Regulated Freelance Solicitor Model' by Paul Bennett
'A Practical Guide to Prison Injury Claims' by Malcolm Johnson
'A Practical Guide to Advising Clients at the Police Station' by Colin Stephen McKeown-Beaumont
'A Practical Guide to Antisocial Behaviour Injunctions – Second Edition' by Iain Wightwick
'Practical Mediation: A Guide for Mediators, Advocates, Advisers, Lawyers, and Students in Civil, Commercial, Business, Property, Workplace, and Employment Cases' by Jonathan Dingle with John Sephton
'The Mini-Pupillage Workbook' by David Boyle
'A Practical Guide to Crofting Law' by Brian Inkster
'A Practical Guide to the Law of Domain Names and Cybersquatting' by Andrew Clemson
'A Practical Guide to the Law of Gender Pay Gap Reporting' by Harini Iyengar
'NHS Whistleblowing and the Law' by Joseph England
'Employment Law and the Gig Economy' by Nigel Mackay & Annie Powell
'A Practical Guide to Noise Induced Hearing Loss (NIHL) Claims' by Andrew Mckie, Ian Skeate, Gareth McAloon
'An Introduction to Beauty Negligence Claims – A Practical Guide for the Personal Injury Practitioner' by Greg Almond
'Intercompany Agreements for Transfer Pricing Compliance' by Paul Sutton
'Zen and the Art of Mediation' by Martin Plowman
'A Practical Guide to Adoption for Family Lawyers' by Graham Pegg

www.ingramcontent.com/pod-product-compliance
Lightning Source LLC
LaVergne TN
LVHW022311200926
848481LV00004B/1287
9781914608612